Curriculum

Poems

Meghan Dunn

Gunpowder Press • Santa Barbara
2021

© 2021 Meghan Dunn

Published by Gunpowder Press
David Starkey, Editor
PO Box 60035
Santa Barbara, CA 93160-0035

Cover Image: Hester Finch, *A Portrait of the Artist as a Young Woman, no. 4* (2017), courtesy of the artist.

ISBN-13: 978-0-9986458-7-2

www.gunpowderpress.com

For my family

and in memory of Sean Brosseau

ACKNOWLEDGEMENTS

With gratitude to the editors of the journals where the following poems first appeared, sometimes in different forms:

The Collagist/ The Rupture: "A Bird in the Hand" and "Epilogue"

Four Way Review: "My Russian Teacher Named Us"

Narrative: "Foreign Language" (as "The Cliff"), "Owen Hart," "Physical Education" (as "Rise"), and "Second Anniversary"

Ploughshares: "Desmond Miller, 1992-2001"

Poetry Northwest: "Drift," "Cartography," "In the Rec Field at Camp Nazareth," "Geometry"(as "The Ring"), "My Students See Emmett Till's Body," and "Seventh Grade Swim Class"

Post Road: "Soap Sirens"

Public Pool: "Chyna" and "Grammar Lesson"

Rock and Sling: "May the Road Rise"

Southern Humanities Review: "Lockdown" and "Historical Context: Two Lesson Plans"

Contents

Drift	11

I.

Geometry	15
Cartography	17
My Russian Teacher Named Us	18
Physical Education	21
Foreign Language	23
Grammar Lesson	25
Lockdown	26

II.

Seventh Grade Swim Class	31
Owen Hart	32
Femur	36
Summer Assignment	37
Historical Context: Two Lesson Plans	40
A Bird in the Hand	41
My Students See Emmett Till's Body	42

III.

Chyna	47
Soap Sirens	48
In the Rec Field at Camp Nazareth	49
Physics Day at Six Flags	51
After a Student's Suicide	53
May the Road Rise	54
Anatomy	55

IV.

When Asked to Consider Awe	61
Curriculum	62
Desmond Miller, 1992-2001	64
Second Anniversary	65
Epilogue	67
Because I Fainted During the Miracle of Life Video in Seventh Grade	68

I stood near the school building and looked in. This is the room where we sat and learned. The windows of a classroom always open to the future, but in our innocence we thought it was only landscape we were seeing from the window.

—*Yehuda Amichai*

Drift

We used to play at witches   My sisters and I
       in our fort of branches with plastic bucket
             brew of twigs pine needles two handfuls

             of earth   Creek water scooped up
     in an old Coke bottle by the back fence
of the nunnery   We weren't scared

we said   But they had a dog
     and he barked like he meant it
         We swirled the water with our fingers

         drank it down that dark sweet
   magic and waited   Now I wake up
with the stick in my hand still

prodding the surface   I think
     about the frailty of the collarbone how
         it holds up our skin like the stays in a shirt

        Years ago my father cut down our fort
   It took him ten minutes   The bare
place left was large enough only

for one   The brown dirt pale
   and dry   It crumbled at my touch   Pine
      needles silvered the ground sharp enough

     to hurt   Where had we brewed
   our potions   This crooked stump   Overgrown
by moss the side of the hill

oozing up around it   Its bark
     scabbed its rings warped   Where
        did we carve our names

I.

Geometry

Dear friend, you're ten years dead.
The world's changed entirely
or not at all, it's hard to say.
The other day, a student who lives
two miles from Lower Manhattan
asked, *What's Wall Street, miss?*

Everything I've taken
for granted... I should
get on my knees right now
to count my blessings,
but I'll stop at one:
I've just come
from my sister's house
where I combed
my nephew's bath-damp hair
against his skull.
On the news, bombs
exploded

on a street where you
and I had walked
in dappled sunlight,
the lindens' shadows
crisscrossing our skin.
Your face, when you looked

at me, was cut in two.
Is this what I see now?
That nowhere is safe?
That nowhere is the place
where nothing's saved?
I'm ten years older than you
never were, still

stroking your loss
like I'd stroke the skin
of my finger after a ring's
been removed. Compressed.
Circumscribed. The skin

thin and soft, closest
to the bone which has narrowed
to accommodate the missing
circle of gold, which I touch
and touch, feeling the shape
of what I can't.

Cartography

This is how we lay at sixteen
on the striped couch in my parent's basement,
TV flickering in the room
where electronics came to die,

knee to knee, elbow
to elbow, your bicep pillowing
my cheek. Our skin the same
temperature. In a cold room,

you were a warm beach.
Ankle to ankle, shin to
shin, and that's all. Nothing
more. We curled together

as maps rolled in a schoolhouse corner,
forgotten, secret to the light
tracing the dust-filled air, seasons
passing outside. Inside the furl,

allies and enemies lay face
to face, almost kissing.
They didn't know that, out here,
their borders were changing,

were all wrong, never existed.

My Russian Teacher Named Us

She named us Yuri and Sergei and Boris.
The first verbs we learned were to smoke, to drink,
to live. We were thirteen years old. We learned

through repetition. I smoke, you smoke,
he or she smokes. We live. She named me Masha,
Mashinka when I was good, Mashka when I was bad,

which was often. We memorized charts
of endings. How neatly the language
fit together, like the nesting dolls

she carried from Russia in a suitcase,
Ded Moroz and his granddaughter
Snegurochka, nestled inside each other.

Everything worth having, according to her,
had been carried from Russia in a suitcase,
except for Levi's jeans and ballpoint pens.

She named me *Slovar*, which means dictionary.
She promised us, one day, she would take us
to Russia, suitcases filled with Levi's jeans.

We could sell them for one hundred USD a pair,
she promised. She never wore jeans.
She wore leather mini-skirts, orange or purple,

and matching turtleneck sweaters with high heels.
She had great legs. She liked to sit sideways
at her desk, legs crossed to one side. She liked

the lights off in the classroom except for
a small desk lamp, its glow circling her head
like a spotlight. She named Steven *Bledny*,

which means pale. She named him Peasant
when he spoke with a Ukrainian accent.
She wore brick red lipstick, a permanent smirk.

One heel dangled from her foot as she crossed
her legs. She liked to tell us the dirt on Peter the Great,
on Anastasia. Her large square glasses shone,

her high rounded perm circled her head
like a halo. She showed us a movie about Rasputin
and the czar's hemophiliac son

and Bledny almost fainted at the nosebleed scene.
She told us how Catherine the Great
had a machine built so she could fuck horses.

She didn't say fuck, but we understood,
or thought we did. She started every story,
I know you think I'm lying. We never

thought she was lying. We chanted after her,
kuda ty idesh. Ya idu domoy. Where are you going?
I'm going home. She promised to tell us

how her family escaped Russia. She used
the word escaped. She promised to tell us
if we all got an A on the quiz

and we did. *I'm not in the mood*, she said.
She was never in the mood. She never
brought us to Russia. In the dark,

she wrote all thirty-six letters on the board
in swirling cursive. She named the letter
she liked best, *the pretty letter*. Once,

when we were bad, she left the classroom.
Through the window, we could see her walking
across the parking lot, her high heels clicking.

She got into her car and drove away.
The lights were off. It was winter outside.
We remembered the song she taught us,

the one she made us sing over and over.
*Pust' vsegda budet solntse, pust' vsegda budet nebo,
pust' vsegda budet Mama, pust' vsegda budu ya.*

*Let there always be sun, let there always be sky,
let there always be Mama, let there always be I.*
Each line had a matching hand movement.

We had practiced it a hundred times.
We believed everything she told us.
Her name was Olga but we never called her that.

We sat in the dark and waited for her.

Physical Education

When he asks me if I'm ready,
I don't even know enough
to know what he means

but I know enough
not to say so. We lie
on his unmade bed

in the basement room,
credits rolling on the movie
we'd watched. His choice.

His hand's at my waist, then on
the part of my belly I fold my hands
over to conceal in photos.

I shift, suck in my stomach
as he peels off my t-shirt to reveal
the bra my mother bought me

from the sales rack at Sears.
Pale pink lace, an imposing row
of hooks in the back

where his hands fumble.
Upstairs, his mother
is baking bread. She'd smiled, said

it would be ready when we
were, that she had real butter too.
Rolling sideways, he's on top,

his knee between my knees, hand
at the button of my jeans, then, inside.
His fingers are cold. He tastes

like the milk his mother poured.
I try to be soft
as butter melting on warm

bread, fat and salt on the tongue.
My mother never told me
all the things I didn't know,

like what to do when his hand
goes to his zipper, when
he's breathing like this

in the dark, when he's rising
like the bread which I smell
above the smell of him,

of me, when I haven't said yes
or no, when I don't understand
the question. I want a mother

to ask me a simple question.
I want to know the answer.
Do you want some bread

*and butter? Would you
like a glass of milk?*

Yes. Yes. Yes.

Foreign Language

I hadn't known Mike but I'd loved
his auburn hair, his fingers inky
from Senior Art, the way he'd leaned
against the bleachers with the stoners

who wore their fathers' old flannels,
drove Le Sabres and Cavaliers,
chain-smoked, and didn't give a shit.
His body in the coffin was the first

I'd ever seen, pale and perfectly
dressed. He'd lost his footing on the cliff
where he'd been climbing with friends,
stumbled, fell, and broke his neck.

Mike's mom shook my hand and thanked me
for coming. His dad gripped my shoulders
a long time, mistaking me, I think,
for someone else. In September,

I was in his French class. He wore a suit
and carried a wood-handled umbrella.
I pictured him strolling through Paris
in the rain. When he gave pop quizzes,

he used our names for the fill-in-the-blanks:
Phillipe adore le football. Marguerite
adore la classe de Monsieur K.
He sang Celine Dion to us in the language lab.

At school, he spoke French to everyone,
even to the janitors and the kids

who took German, and when I saw him
at the grocery store, he stopped me

and my mother to exclaim *Quelle belle tomates*!
while I kept saying *Oui, oui,* because
it was all I knew. Each September
we returned to him, older, more like Mike,

and saddened him a little more. He yelled
at us in English for talking after the bell,
or for tossing, from one side of the room
to the other, the straw donkey the Spanish class had left.

He spoke English when he talked about Mike,
who was dead, and about his students,
who were lazy and didn't want to work.
In French 4, we could never answer him

fast enough. *So you don't want to work?*
he'd say, slamming his book. *Well, I don't want
to work either.* I think of him on these
bitter days, so cold the sun glances off

the iced windows of the bus and it seems
we're barreling through a dense tunnel of wind
and light. I hope I never see him again,
never run into him at the supermarket,

never again buy ripe tomatoes beaded
with moisture. What could I possibly say,
standing in the aisle speaking a language
indecipherable to us both?

Grammar Lesson

After school, Carl asks me to read an essay he's written
about walking with his father in Haiti when he was six.
They walked to the port after church, the sun hot
on their bare heads, his father pausing
to wipe his face with a red handkerchief.
When they arrived, there were men shouting, running,
men with machetes which they waved in the air above their heads.
He and his father hid behind a fruit stand,
its counter heaped high with mangoes and plantains,
and his father covered Carl's ears
but he saw people lying on the ground.
"Peoples heads," he wrote, "were lying on the ground too."

Is this real, I ask, and he nods.
Small for his age, thin and frail,
his neck seems too slender
to support his head, his long-lashed eyes.
This should be possessive, I say.
The heads belong to the people.
In a different version of this story, he looks back at me.
Not anymore, he says.
In a different version of this story, I listen.
In that version, his head isn't bowed over the paper
as I lift my red pen to the page,
add the small machete swoop
of the apostrophe.

Lockdown

1.
When the alarm goes off, they file to the corner
furthest from door and window, any shooter's angle,
while I scan the hall and lock the door,
hang a paper over the square of glass in its center,
shut off the lights. In the dark, we listen
for the boots of the school safety agents,
the door handle jiggling as they check
their list of the ways that we'll stay safe.
The intercom clicks on to say it's over,
and James raises his hand.

2.
We're starting *Antigone*.
The state is sick, James reads,

You and your principles are to blame.
The alarm rings, so we file

ourselves down, become small
as possible, orderly. On the news,

a Black boy raises his hands over his head
and he is shot twelve times,

left to lie in the street, uncovered.
A white jury decides there's no crime.

The students plan a walkout and a white teacher asks,
Why a walkout, isn't school the way to avoid this?

This.
Shot while Black, while unarmed, while hands

overhead, the signal teachers taught meant,
I am friendly, don't shoot.

The city sends an email:
The children will have feelings,

it says. *Acknowledge them.*
It also says, *no walkout.*

I lock the doors and keep them in.

3.
The class blames Kreon for everything.
They raise their hands in disgust,

James' hands casting a black shadow on the white wall.
Another teacher says, *If the anger was productive,*

it'd be different. In Scene III,
Haimon pleads with his father.

Be different this once, James reads
and looks at me. This isn't a drill.

I think of the boy falling, the heaviness
of his body, the lightness of the air

rushing through the twelve holes,
the dust which blankets him without care.

There is such perfection in what we've been given,
the way all cameras attempt to approximate

the human eye. His friends said what they saw
but no one believed them.

Words are a blunt tool.

4.
If the child is caught
outside the locked door,
we are told, we cannot
open it, that the child instead
should face the wall, should
turn his face to the cold
tile of the hallway and raise
his hands above his head.
This, we are told, is a signal
for when help comes. His hands
above his head, his face
turned to the wall: these say
I am friendly, these say,
don't shoot, this
is what we teach them.
We ask what to tell the children.
What do we say?
They will have feelings, we are told.
Acknowledge them.

II.

Seventh Grade Swim Class

We pull school bathing suits from the bin in the girls' locker room,
skirted, inelastic, color-coded by size. I don't know who designed them
but my first guess is a sadist in the early 1950s. My second guess is a man.

I'm a small girl so I wear pine green, not as small as Courtney
who wears red, not nearly as large as Melissa who is eggplant.
No one in this class wears black. We are a rainbow of hideousness

as we line up on the deck to study one another's emerging curves,
make note of who is lacking, who has too much, who is just right.
Slumped on benches poolside are the girls with their periods

or mothers willing to write notes saying they have their periods.
I envy them, sweating sullenly in their street clothes, as we wade in,
butterfly and breaststroke to the whistle of Mrs. J, our gym teacher,

married to Mr. J, the earth science teacher who slips images
of their New Mexico vacations into the slide carousel between igneous
and metamorphic. This is how I know she can smile.

Now, she lies on the damp tile and kicks like a Reebok-clad frog,
as we cough our way down the lanes, suits loosening around us,
the bellies and breasts slackening in folds the way our own skin will

one day, the chlorinated water rushing through the softened seams,
bringing us both forward and back in time: We are babies floating
in our mothers' wombs. We are old women floating in our own skin.

We are, please God, anywhere but here
in these unknowable,
these terrifying forms.

Owen Hart

The delivery guys gasp and gather
around the TV, jostle each other
to see Owen face-down in the ring,
one arm cactused upward.

I'm in the back room at Tony's Pizza
folding boxes when he falls.
Kansas City shouts. Claps.
The announcer says: *this is not*

entertainment, this is
as real as real can be,
folks. The crowd on their feet,
children perched on parents'

shoulders. Flashbulbs,
70,000 cameras pinning
him to the mat with light.
I'm sixteen, all eyes and ears,

a body I haven't tried, a mouth
I don't use in the dark of the back room,
where the delivery guys and I breathe
together, one big, stupid organism

in red, white, and green hats.
We're not allowed to stand around.
I wait for Sue to yell at us, tell us
to go make her some money.

But all I hear is the TV, the sigh
of the ovens, Casey Kasem
on the radio by the register.
On the TV, Owen Hart is dying.

The eye we can see
is open, his mouth too, open
to the scent of the mats: leather,
sweat, ammonia, something

he remembers from childhood.
He can't see the crowd now.
He can't hear them chant
his name, the murmur

like a wave: *this is
real, this is real,
this, this, this,
real, real, real.*

He is wheeled away.
Someone wipes the mat.
In the dining room,
the Genesee Light clock

ticks above empty booths.
The phone rings. Two large
double cheese. On the TV,
someone taps out.

Later tonight, one of the guys climbs
to the low roof of the restaurant,

spreads his drunken arms (*for Owen,*
he shouts) and leaps belly-first

onto the picnic table below.
Years later, he emails me a video
and a part of me I'm ashamed
of clicks to open it: Owen

in the rafters about to descend,
in a blue singlet, a superhero cape.
A gag, something he's done
a hundred times before. Only this time,

he falls. This time,
I know it's coming.
My muscles tense.
My mouth open.

Like a dummy. He falls.
Like he's dead even before he dies.
When he hits the mat, he bounces.
His cape doesn't have time

to flutter, to catch the air
before he lands hard in the ring
and is still and doesn't move
except his head, back and forth

a little bit against the leather.
His mouth open and then
it shuts, tasting
the air, thick with sweat

and beer and popcorn
and what is the smell? He can
almost think, it was
something his father used

to oil the mats in the barn
where he and his brothers wrestled
as kids, all knees and elbows
and wanting and not wanting

to hurt each other. The hay
in its bales and the stray pieces
loose and floating in the light.
The two horses shuffling

in their stalls. Underneath
his brothers' sharp sweat,
something else, an oil
that, if he could rub his fingers

together, he would remember
its texture, its mineral sheen
on the whorls of his fingers,
still raw from the mat, his brother's skin.

If he could open his mouth, he could taste it.

Femur

The first and only time I saw a human bone pierce through
the skin that housed it, I was underwater, looking up
through the scratched lenses of my goggles.

Sinking slowly, I watched the ripples I'd made
in my leap from the deep end diving board
edging outwards, closer and closer to the tiled sides

of the pool. There was a rule about getting out of the way,
clearing the area underneath the board after you jumped,
but I wanted to see when the circles I'd made would break,

and so I was still underneath when the next girl jumped.
I half-saw the double-bounce, the bobble, the girl flying up,
then coming down sideways, her thigh hitting the edge

of the board as she crashed into the water, breaking
the ripples I'd created, her leg twisted into an L, her blood
spiraling out around us in loose concentric circles.

Then, the slash of the lifeguard diving in.
By the time I made it out, they had her flat on the deck.
The jagged end of her femur pointed skyward.

My mother, the nurse, knelt next to her as if she didn't notice
that the inside of the girl's body was on the outside.
Speaking calmly, blood puddling around them,

spreading across the concrete to where I stood dripping.
My mother leaned in. I took a step backward.
And then another. And another. I cleared the area.

I got out of the way.

Summer Assignment

> To prepare for our upcoming study of American literature, please use your own experience to consider the question, *What does it mean to be American?* 500-750 words.

On the last day of school, I copy it on clean white
paper and pass it out to my students
in their neat rows and the rainbowed curve
of their necks bending over their desks,

as they scramble for pens and highlighters
to mark the most important details,
the way their eyes turn to me after reading,
awaiting instruction, their compliance

which will not protect them, their desire
to be right and do well, their existential
anxiety, is as American, as heartbreaking
and infuriating, as anything else

I have seen in my own limited life,
more American than anything
I am capable of dreaming or being.
All summer, they email me with questions.

*So sorry to bother you, but can I write
about police brutality in America?
Is this what you mean by national issues?*
Yes, I write back. *Yes, exactly.*

You are on the right track.
Another student writes, *I hate to interrupt*

*your summer vacation, however, is it possible
for me to talk about how I am not an American?*

*Is that fine, can I write like that,
or do I have to make myself an American
and sort of brag about it?*
I am at a lake house in the Berkshires

when I open this email. It's July 4th.
After replying (*Yes, this is fine.
The assignment is open to interpretation,
as students will have different thoughts and experiences.*),

I close the laptop and go down to the dock
where fireworks are exploding into the sky,
red and white and blue and gold bursting
against the purple sky and gray smoke, their light,

their exuberant violence rippling outwards
in the blackened mirror of the lake.
What does it mean to be American?
I go up to the house and open my laptop again,

planning to quote from Thomas Jefferson.
*Life, liberty, and the pursuit of happiness.
We can do better*, I plan to write
but I see a former student has already posted

this quote. *LMFAOOO*, she's written.
Right. Let's start with life.
Out the window, I can see children with sparklers
twirling with dizzy abandon on the lawn,

the sparklers hissing and spitting golden light
from their pale hands, children allowed
to play with fire, to write their names
on the darkening sky.

Historical Context: Two Lesson Plans

1.
My students study the lynching photos,
study the smiles on the faces of onlookers,
the postcards plastered with the images
mailed to relatives with greetings, expressions,
even, of love. The men in the photos, the murderers,
they thought they were saving their women, their children,
from something. They thought they had a good reason
for what they did. I study the faces of my students
studying the photos. I too think I have a good reason.

2.
When showing a documentary, I tell my students
I'll say when to shut their eyes.
Ten minutes in, a girl starts crying.
You said you'd tell us when to shut our eyes, she sobs.
On the screen, a man hangs from a tree.
The family below him smiles.
The small boy sits on his father's shoulders,
his blond hair almost brushing
the feet of the hanged man.
My student is still crying.
Close your eyes, I say.

A Bird in the Hand

A bird in the hand, my mother always says.
But I think it depends on the bird and the hand
and the nature of the holding.
And in this lesson, am I the bird or the hand?
The bird placid, easy to catch.
The hand greedy, snatching at anything bright.
Either way, an insult.
There's more dignity in being the bird,
but this may be another way I am wrong.
Meanwhile, let's not forget about those birds in the bush.
So in love with the bird in hand, its small heart
under our thumb, it's easy to forget them,
those birds. But they're still out there,
neither caught nor catching,
not together but neither alone,
slender claws gripping slender twigs,
sidling to the bough's bend, which dips
them to the stream where they drink
and fly away
and never return.

My Students See Emmett Till's Body

They don't look away,
though I've warned that there's no
shame in turning their heads,
that when Emmett's mother says
People should see, they will see
what they can't un-see. The shape
above the buttoned collar of the shirt,
what is it? The nose is what gives it away,
makes it plain that this is a face
of a boy their age. Gabriel in the back row
touches his own nose lightly
with his own brown finger.
He traces its edges
while Jasmine frames her face
with her hands, covers her eyes
and mouth, then uncovers them
to see how Emmett's nose orients
the other features of his face,
provides a center to the swelling,
now they see, of the cheek,
his mouth, now they see it,
it's a mouth. Davina's mouth
is a pressed-tight line.
When she turns to me, her eyes
are wells of un-knowing.
I don't know what she's thinking.
Tonight I'll go home and look
at my own face in the mirror.
I won't know what I'm thinking
except that I have a nose
that no one wants to hack

from my face, skin the color
of cottonseed mixed with blood,
the white of a mother's red-rimmed eye.
I have a neck no one wants
to barb or break, a face that
a white man would break
a Black boy's neck for looking at
too long or in the wrong way
or not at all.
I have two eyes to look
at whatever I want, a mouth,
unbroken teeth, a tongue,
a voice I don't know
what to do with. But if I knew
how to whistle, wouldn't I?

III.

Chyna

Beast, the boys say,
over the roar of Monday Night Raw,
but I think she is a bear,
black haired and brutal, comfortable
in her oiled flesh, which she wears like a custom suit.
Large, somehow lithe,
she sidesteps her opponents' swings
in her black leather boots.
She fights men.
Beast, the boys say,
steroid freak,
as she lifts a man high,
wraps his thighs around her face,
smashes him spine-first into the mat.
He struggles to stand
while she waits to toss him across the ring
like the nothing he seems to her.
One of the boys makes a fist.
He pounds it into the cup of his other hand
like he's churning butter.
I wouldn't fuck that with your dick, he says,
to another boy, who laughs,
puts his hand on my thigh.
I love the way she moves,
how she fills up her whole body.
Inside my small frame, I am even smaller,
and in this room, a kind of decoration,
a reassurance of what is right and natural.
Onscreen, Chyna bends a man in half
and the boys' faces twitch
with everything they hate
and don't understand.

Soap Sirens

My mother knew each family's secret:
each cheating tycoon and gold digger half-sister
whose illegitimate son was switched at birth.
During love scenes, my sisters and I snuck peeks
through our fingers. When the music trailed off,
my mother allowed us to look again.
I dreamed of eight weddings like the heroine,
each more special than the last, and the chance
to attend my own funeral in disguise,
unrecognizable beneath dark glasses, a darker wig.
Who would throw herself on my grave
and sob, who would come to claw at the earth?
And when my character came back from the dead,
who would replace me, strolling in one day
with a better body, a more musical voice?
Today, the role of Meghan will be played by...
I shared my name with three girls at school,
but the soaps swarmed with Biancas,
Kendalls, and Simones, who strode around
like predatory angels in strapless dresses
and three-inch heels, and their curls fluttered
as if a slight breeze blew wherever they alighted.
When they thrashed about on satin sheets with men,
all interchangeable Kens, their shoulder blades jutted
from their taut flesh like bony wings.
I wanted their lives: to be rescued from a rabid dog
or a runaway Buick with suspicious brakes,
to fall victim to a maniac's plot,
or have my memory erased by the evil Dr. N.
I wanted to disappear, to die and be reborn
like them, with a different face,
an immaculate new mind.

In the Rec Field at Camp Nazareth

Me, on my stomach in the long grass,
and you on my back, the seat

of triumph, my legs bent in defeat
over your shoulders. My cheek

to the ground, I've got an ant's eye
view of ants. You've pinned me

with the Walls of Jericho, a submission
move and I submit. I submit

to mid-August, to the grass brown
and going on forever, one long blade

that bisects my eye. On one side
of my vision, the ants scurry

from their hole, spiraling out
over the pockmarked dirt

as they escape, their patent leather
thoraxes shining in the same sun

that shines on me, makes me squint
my skyward eye and arch my back and still

my lungs as I curse your steady
breath, your strong hands, and curl

my own fingers into the dead
grass, startling again the ants,

who also will not yield,
already rebuilding the home

we've destroyed. They carry
only what they need: some rocks,

a crumb of bread, the eggs that,
cloud-like, line their legs, even

the bodies of their dead, which
they bury in the sandy earth,

grain by grain, circling madly
until no shine is seen.

Physics Day at Six Flags

We boarded the Viper, accelerometers in hand.
        Armed with courage, #2 pencils, a plan
to hold someone's hand. At the first loop, we forgot it all,

flung our arms in the air, compasses and graphing calculators
        raining down on the crowds below. We got sunburned,
sick on cotton candy, sick on the Gravitron, which failed

to make us weightless. Before the trip, our teacher
        had weighed us, so our calculations would be correct.
He wrote our names and weights on a chart

and stuck it on the wall behind his desk. We tried not to look
        but we could feel it there at the back of the room.
On the bus home, we frantically filled in the worksheets

we'd neglected. *If Anna is riding the Viper*
        and she is moving at 19 miles per second through the curve
of the loop, how does Newton's 2nd law apply?

What did you get, everyone whispered, and whatever
        the smartest person said, we all wrote it down.
We didn't know anything but we knew that it made sense.

There were laws that governed everything.
        Laws of motion, laws of gravity, laws
about where to sit in the cafeteria, whose hand could reach

for whose across the back row of the bus. We filled in
        the worksheets. We didn't know the answers.
I wondered: *If the bus is hurtling forward at 57 miles per hour*

and three of us will be dead in three years,
  how does Newton's 1st law apply?
There was an external force

but we didn't know its name. Our calculations
  were not correct. We tried not to look.
We could feel it at the back of the room. It knew

all our weights, could tell when
  we were objects in motion,
when we would become objects at rest.

After a Student's Suicide

Useless anyway, all these thoughts of why,
of what we could have noticed and did not.
Better we should contemplate the sky,

which has no answers, but a blue our eyes
can rest on, comprehend, a simpler knot.
Useless anyway, all these thoughts of why.

Instead, let us consider this day's light,
a brilliance we know cannot be caught.
Better. Let us contemplate the sky,

the sun in its clear and limited supply,
the shadows it designs, the expected night.
Useless anyway, all these thoughts: why,

what we could have noticed, a cracked gaze,
a leaving glance, an away-ness in her throat.
No. Better we should contemplate the sky.

Not the child with her serious smile,
her shy light, her meticulous thought...
Useless anyway, all these thoughts of why.
Better we should contemplate the sky.

May the Road Rise

for Uncle Pat

Though it's said that God is saddened
by your kind, I hope he knelt to cup you
as you fell. I hope you never felt its burn,
the cord which tugged around your neck.
I hope you were saved, at least, from that.

What if the basement floor had risen
and the chair you stood on
had been borne up lightly, just in time,
lifting you out from that cellar, past your wife
who dozed on the living room sofa,

above even the roof you'd promised to re-shingle,
over the darkened mills and frost-tipped fields
of upstate NY, higher and higher
until the world lay below, the way you saw it
as a boy, in photographs taken from space

and printed in the *National Geographics* you collected,
the globe reduced to blue and green, earth
and space, seen and unseen, so far away
you wouldn't see us, tiny, waving.

Anatomy

A student in my 5th period class tells me the noose
in the image we're studying is a trigger.
He looks out the window as we discuss the image,
the noose, what it tells us about the character
it encircles. Sometimes, I think, it reveals nothing.
Sometimes the only window to gaze out of
is my own blue eye. It looks forward
and back, in the living room
where I sit with my family on Easter
watching the *Passion of the Christ* on TV.
On the screen, Judas looks us all in the eye
and the noise he makes I won't describe.

*

Hanged, I say, correcting a student.
When you're talking about a man.

*

On the thirteenth card, the Hanged Man,
a man hangs from a T shaped tree.
The calm expression on his face,
his hands hidden behind his back:
these indicate he is not struggling.
He has chosen to do this. The Hanged Man
willingly gives up his existence.
This is symbolized by the halo around his head.

*

"To suicide" is not a verb, I tell the class.
To commit, I say and write it on the board.
The suicide is the object, not the action, I say.
*Jocasta, Antigone, Eurydice, Haimon, Dido—
our subjects, the ones doing the action.*
I circle the parts of speech.
A girl in the back calls out, *Miss.*
We should read happier books, she says.

*

Earlier, we'd gathered around the table for Easter dinner,
around the empty chair, where my uncle,
my father's younger brother, would have sat,
if he hadn't, thirteen days before,
from a T shaped beam in his basement,
hung himself. He chose to do this.

*

On the TV, Judas is finally dead.
He looks out from the screen
and what I see in his eyes is not relief
but a reflection of the living
room where I sit with my family.
I scan the room, my sister avoids my gaze,
my mother swirls her drink.
I don't look at my father
but I can feel his presence
the way I feel my own heart,
huge and erratic and full of questions.

*

Reverse the card, my friend tells me, it has a new meaning.
Unknot yourself, Judas.
Open your arms and ascend.
Reverse yourself, uncle.
Make that beam a plank on which you balance.
Fathers, lift your children to watch
as the hanged man ascends to the top of the tree
as the rope unknots itself from his throat.

IV.

When Asked to Consider Awe

When asked to consider awe, I think first of the sky,
and then of the ocean, stranger and more terrifying
and thus more beautiful, and then of an article I read

about the color blue, a color that humans
evolved to see, a color we weren't born knowing.
The author of the article cites ancient languages,

tracing the order colors appear in their lexicon,
Homer's description of the wine-dark sea,
which I had read as poetry, but which the author

ascribes to a deficit of words, an inability to describe
a shade you have no language for, the impossibility
of seeing the blueness of a sky, a sea, the bed

of someone's fingernails without the words to connect
the eye to the brain. And this in turn makes me think
of my father, who while playing golf, suddenly put his hand

to his left eye. A curtain, he said, a black curtain
coming down over half his vision as the retina pasted
to the back of his eyeball began to lift, to peel at the edges

like the stickers they put on fruit at the supermarket.
Is this how badly made we are?
And yet, within an hour, he was at the doctor's office,

awake in the chair as they spooned his eye from its socket,
stitched his retina back in place, the surgeon's face appearing
as if from behind a curtain, inverted, in the small black dot of his eye.

Curriculum

Even the cicadas were dying from heat
and the brown lake looked life-giving

as the mouth of God, something I wanted
to be swallowed by. Yet the dock's cool slats

were deserted, no one swung her legs
through the dark water, no one dipped a toe.

Priests came, social workers, even after
the police removed the tape from the beach,

they kept coming. Our teacher came too,
with faux Zen calm, familiar sheaves of paper.

For each tragedy, she had pre-printed
solace. *Grief is like the wind*, said one page.

Another, inked with borders of fall foliage,
whispered, *Death is nothing at all.*

I have only slipped into the next room.
My friend Sean, who blew his good deep breath

into the lungs of the drowned child, pushed
away her papers. Soon he too

was dead, tossed to the shoulder
of a Tennessee highway, and it was not

nothing and our grief was nothing like
the wind. Again, she xeroxed passages

from Corinthians, *Chicken Soup
for the Soul*. One Christmas,

she'd found her own son at the roadside,
packages crushed in his arms.

She lived to keep the lights lit
in his window above the garage.

She lived.

Desmond Miller, 1992-2001

Camp Nazareth, Woodgate, NY

I imagine he sank like copper,
but I wasn't there
when they pulled him out.
I only know the splintered dock
where they laid his featherweight,
and the way Keith's hands shook
hours later, still cool from cradling him
beneath the dark bulk of the Palisades.
Now, autumn falls around us,
the color of blood and pumpkin.
I keep him there, face-up
in the shallows. His eyes widen
at the spiral of an oak leaf,
a rowboat's gliding thump.
At night, the lake murmurs
around him. Already, winter approaches.
Someday the earth will spin backwards
and August will begin again,
a sunlit dagger, where we dive
deep and fast.

Second Anniversary

Today, June 10th, is the day for all who loved you
to gather in the park and raise money in your name.

Somewhere in town, a boy who matches
your description plays guitar and doesn't care

if his homework gets done, a teenage boy luckier
than you. But for the moment, there's Utica Club

and Mexican food, plenty of cake, the kind
of party you'd have thrown, but quieter, more subdued,

though we do our best to cheerfully tell old stories,
play your CDs, Nirvana, the Allman Brothers, the Dead.

The sheet cake's iced with your picture, and your mother
makes sure everyone has a piece. I eat

your shoulder, blue shirt, the neck of your Les Paul.
The day you bought it, you strapped it across my chest,

solid body electric, twelve whole pounds.
When I close my eyes, I still feel its weight.

The man none of us will mention, the driver
of the truck that killed you, I wonder how he

marks this anniversary. Did he lie awake last night,
dreading the morning, the hour he gets up

to bow his head over breakfast, pack his children
off to school, head out to Knoxville or Birmingham,

loaded with milk or bread, some ordinary cargo?
If his route brings him by that spot today, five miles

to the Chattanooga exit, is he taken back
to when he was a man heading home, almost

off work, singing along to Freebird on the radio,
unburdened as we all feel near quitting time, too careless

to check his mirrors before changing lanes?
I imagine he pulls over today to the side of the highway

where you died and leans his forehead against the hot dash
to suffer again the sirens and car horns, the surreal drift

of the helicopter landing, then lifting you away.
Or maybe he doesn't and, Sean, what difference does it make?

Something in me needs to believe that your absence
is felt beyond this small-town park, our forced cheer,

that you are mourned along the length of 81 South,
and that when your strong heart stopped beating,

something else in the world stood still too: a bee
balanced on the lip of a lily, or a woman who'd pricked

herself sewing calmed by the tiny welling of blood.
Each small pause built, until a swath of silence

cut across the heartland, rendering us all mute,
awed by the hush, which a single word could break.

Epilogue

A little advice, too late:
Love what you can carry.
Such as, a smooth oddly-shaped stone,
a small pet, a child who never grows.
Love, we never told each other
the truth. Such as, the time you hurt me
still hurts. Such as, the time I hurt you
hurts more. Some things I will never forgive.
Such as, the cold side of the bed.
The undented pillow.
The time you said, *I hope you find*
someone to make you happy.
The time I forgot and I was happy.
Such as, today. Love,
there was too much of you to count.
The place we loved is gone.
You know the one I mean.
What I mean is, it's still there
but the sky enrages me.
Never the long grass. Never again
those crickets. Never the murmur of your voice
against the unfair backdrop of goldenrod.
Never the navy sky.
Shut up, sky. Stop the twinkling
that no one's left to see. Never again
the darkening we failed to notice.

Because I Fainted During the Miracle of Life Video in Seventh Grade

I never saw the birth and no one would describe it to me
when I emerged from the nurse's office, the other girls

giggling knowingly, their hands to their mouths,
while the ice pack I held pressed to the nape of my neck

melted into the loose ends of my ponytail.
I had to imagine it instead. I pictured a tunnel

the color of my flushed cheeks, the smooth cool
of the linoleum against my face, the murmur

of the class coming into focus around me.
I didn't know where the tunnel went or why,

but I knew it was something miraculous.
Something to change me.

Years later, it was light when I got on the train
and when we emerged from the tunnel, it was dark.

We were on the bridge, high above the river,
the air frozen on the train windows in shattered

circles, my face looking back at me from the glass,
lines around my eyes like little knives. I was old.

My whole life had happened already.
But somewhere in the reflection was the girl

returning to class, the nurse's office pass crumpled
in her damp palm, waiting to be filled in, to learn

what she'll give birth to, not knowing yet it's herself,
over and over again, the pain cresting and falling,

pushing and crying out until she holds herself,
bloodied, in her arms, finally,

the miracle she's been waiting for.

Author's Note

Thank you to the Bread Loaf Writers' Conference, especially Michael Collier, Jennifer Grotz, Noreen Cargill, and Jason Lamb, for your support and the community you have built.

To the Sewanee Writers' Conference, the Fine Arts Work Center in Provincetown, the St. Botolph Club Foundation, and the Writers' Room of Boston for your support of my work.

To everyone at Brooklyn Poets, especially Jason Koo, Jessica Greenbaum, and Patricia Spears Jones.

To everyone who read and gave feedback on these poems.

To all my teachers, especially Sue Roberts, John Skoyles, Daniel Tobin, David Baker, Alan Shapiro, Van Jordan, Ellen Bryant Voigt, Eavan Boland, and Ross Gay for your advice and your example. For seeing me and these poems and for making both better.

To David Starkey and Chryss Yost at Gunpowder Press, for your care and dedication in bringing this book to print. To Jessica Jacobs for selecting this manuscript and for your generous description of the work. To Hester Finch for the beautiful cover art.

To the many friends whose love and support made this book possible and made its writing, often, a joy: to Keith Wilson, for your insight and generosity, for your big heart and all your emails with brilliant edits. To Allison Albino, for the tête-à-têtes and the deviled eggs. To Jamey Hatley and Jessamine Chan, for these years of friendship, understanding, and the group chat. To Cam Terwilliger and Cara Blue Adams, for being excellent neighbors and even better friends. To Donna Spruijt-Metz, Silvia Bonilla, Michelle Peñaloza, Chaney Kwak, and Keith Leonard for your friendship and support.

To Emily Barrett, Diana Gilberti, Connie Johnson, Shannon Toumey, and Michael Foley. To Sara Zogby and Adrianne Greer. To Dave Mehl. To Christine Willis and Vivian Roman. To my book club, especially Meredith Mann, Dawn Miller, and Katie Tuss.

To my fellow teachers, especially Paulina Murton, Ben Spencer, Holly Fritz, Betsy Bowman, Becky Wilusz, John Vircillo, Colin Marshall, Amy Mogulescu, Evan Focht, Katherine Clark, Joanna Beer, and Jennifer Glaser. In loving memory of Kimarlee Nguyen, whose joy at seeing this book in print I can so easily picture.

Thank you to my students, for your grace and your brilliance.

To my extended family for your unending enthusiasm and support. To my brothers-in-law, Matt and Pete. To my nieces and nephews: Maggie, Howie, Ceci, Sean, Alex, and Rita.

To my sisters, Beth and Jenny, for your wisdom and patience. For understanding me. For being my two favorite people in the world.

To my parents, for giving me space to read and dream. For making everything possible. I love you. Thank you.

About the Poet

Meghan Dunn lives in Brooklyn, New York, where she teaches high school English. Her work has appeared in *Ploughshares*, *Narrative*, *Poetry Northwest*, *Four Way Review*, and *Southern Humanities Review*, among others. She is a four-time recipient of scholarships from the Bread Loaf Writers' Conference and a 2019 Tennessee Williams Scholar at the Sewanee Writers' Conference. Her website is http://meghandunnpoet.com

Barry Spacks Poetry Prize Series

2015
Instead of Sadness
Catherine Abbey Hodges

2016
Burning Down Disneyland
Kurt Olsson

2017
Posthumous Noon
Aaron Baker

2018
The Ghosts of Lost Animals
Michelle Bonczek Evory

2019
Drinking with O'Hara
Glenn Freeman

2020
Curriculum
Meghan Dunn

Also from Gunpowder Press

The Tarnation of Faust: Poems by David Case

Mouth & Fruit: Poems by Chryss Yost

Shaping Water: Poems by Barry Spacks

Original Face: Poems by Jim Peterson

What Breathes Us: Santa Barbara Poets Laureate, 2005-2015
Edited by David Starkey

Unfinished City: Poems by Nan Cohen

Raft of Days: Poems by Catherine Abbey Hodges

Mother Lode: Poems by Peg Quinn

and the Shoreline Voices Projects:

Buzz: Poets Respond to SWARM
Edited by Nancy Gifford and Chryss Yost

Rare Feathers: Poems on Birds & Art
Edited by Nancy Gifford, Chryss Yost, and George Yatchisin

To Give Life a Shape: Poems Inspired by the Santa Barbara Museum of Art
Edited by David Starkey and Chryss Yost

www.ingramcontent.com/pod-product-compliance
Lightning Source LLC
Chambersburg PA
CBHW030457010526
44118CB00011B/983